MW00364646

WEDDING TIPS
FOR
Grooms

JAMES HARRISON

summersdale

Contents

———◆———

Introduction

Congratulations! You're getting married and the big day is fast approaching. Compared to the proposal, you probably think getting married will be a breeze. And, as exciting and fun as it is, the planning can be time-consuming, stressful and nerve-wracking (if not for you, then definitely for your partner). The wedding day, however, should be none of these things. It should be exciting, exhilarating and ever-so-slightly emotional, filled with love and laughter, and ending with a party to end all parties.

Being a groom is never as simple as just showing up. Even if you weren't involved in the planning, there are plenty of ways you can dodge disaster, impress your love and contribute to the success of the wedding on the day. This book is the holy grail of groom guidance and it's got you covered from the night before you say 'I do!' right up until the honeymoon suite. So put the champagne on ice, call your bestest of men and prepare to enjoy the most wonderful, worry-free wedding day of your life.

The night before

After years of living the single dream, then dating the person of your dreams, tomorrow is the day you say "I do" to a real lifetime of love. Get your head in the game and think like a pro-footballer the night before the big match to avoid getting blotto or sleeping in.

The right mindset

Get your silliness out of your system.
Tomorrow is a very important day with
serious implications. Yes, it should be
fun, but unless your partner is marrying
you specifically for your fart jokes, it's a
good idea to de-silly yourself the night
before. Hang out with mates, watch your
favourite comedy show and start giggling.
It will also give those abs a workout and
help you to relax.

It's OK to have butterflies in your stomach. Just get them to fly in formation.

— ROB GILBERT

The last supper

You're not spending your last night on death row before facing Ol' Sparky, so don't treat your last unmarried dinner as an opportunity to expand your waistline. You might not care if your breath still smells of garlic or if you spend your wedding day excusing yourself because of a dodgy curry the night before, but your partner probably will.

Last-minute preparation

- If you're feeling nervous, that's perfectly normal. Talk through any worries you might have with a close mate or relative, and you'll soon realise you're just really, really excited!

- Cut all the tags off any new clothes that you or your groomsmen are going to be wearing, and make sure everything is pressed to perfection.

♦ Read through your wedding vows if you've written them yourself (or write them if you've left it to the last minute!) – it will help to refocus your mind on what the whole day is going to be about. Similarly, take a look over your wedding speech to make sure you remember to thank everyone.

♦ Try not to call your spouse-to-be; it will make the grand reveal of seeing them the next day all the more special. If you can't resist, send them a special message to tell them how you feel.

Don't forget...

Spend three minutes or so going through your wedding checklist of all the items you need to remember for the next day. Make sure you know where the following things are located:

- Your full wedding-day outfit, whether that be a traditional suit (two or three pieces) with shirt and tie/cravat, or a kilt, a kimono, or a T-shirt and shorts

- Accessories (cufflinks, handkerchief, braces, hat, etc.)

- Buttonhole (is this being delivered the following day or are you getting it at the venue?)
- Shoes (with accompanying socks)
- Underpants (if you have a lucky pair then make sure they're clean!)
- The wedding rings
- Wallet and other personal items (phone, etc.)
- Jacket and an umbrella, just in case
- Any other items, e.g. any alternative clothing, wedding vows, wedding speech, any gifts (e.g. for the groomsmen, flower girls, etc.).

It's a declaration to the world that you'll hold each other's hands for ever.

♦ ——— PRUE LEITH ON MARRIAGE

I love you because the entire universe conspired to help me find you.

PAULO COELHO

Sleep like a king

Getting a good night's sleep before the big day will make sure you look and feel your best when it matters. Don't let butterflies get the better of you with these sleep-tastic tips.

* Get in a good workout at some point during the day. That way your muscles will feel relaxed and ready to rest.

* Wind down early by chilling out however you choose after dinner.

- Turn the lights down low and sip on a cup of camomile tea or warm milk (go on, we won't judge). Failing that, a shot of your best whisky will do the trick.

- Take a hot shower.

- If you can, avoid relying on sleeping pills or drinking too much alcohol – these could affect you negatively the next day.

Disaster dodger

While it may not take you hours to get ready, you don't want to underestimate how long you'll need and feel rushed tomorrow. Make sure you set an alarm, giving yourself more than enough time to be able to enjoy your last morning of unwedded bliss.

In love the paradox occurs that two beings become one and yet remain two.

ERICH FROMM

*A good marriage
is like a casserole:
only those responsible
for it really know
what goes in it.*

◆ ——————— ANONYMOUS

◆ ——————————— *Notes*

Wakey-wakey!

Like a kid on Christmas morning,
you're waking up to a day of marvellous
magic. Keep your cool, go with the
flow and don't panic. This morning
is all about relaxing and prepping
yourself for your partner.

A little help

Your groomsmen made sure your stag-do was one you'll probably never be able to fully remember. Now's the time to make sure they help you deliver a day you'll never forget. Unmarried mates will be a bit bewildered by what you're about to do, and married ones will know what's going through your groomy mind, so harness their help and support to make sure things run smoothly.

Breakfast of champions

Before any fun and frolics take place, your stomach and the hardy tummies of your bestest men need lining. Prepare a plentiful fry-up feast with all the trimmings before any Dutch courage comes your way and you're guaranteed to make it to the ceremony with a full platoon of suited and booted buddies.

Setting the mood

- While you want to get ready in plenty of time, don't get dressed too soon – otherwise you'll end up with a baked beans stain on your crisp white shirt.

- If you want to have a drink, have it before you get to the ceremony venue – there's nothing as unclassy as a gentlemanly groom standing outside the venue holding a beer can.

- Get the party started with your favourite tunes or play some video games with the guys to keep the mood relaxed.

*Marriage is
a language of love,
equality and inclusion.*

EVAN WOLFSON

Don't forget...

It's OK to be romantic. If your partner's given you a little gift or card to open on the day, don't be embarrassed to do it in front of your mates. If anything, it will help them better understand why you're saying goodbye to your bachelor days. Likewise, why not do one of the following to make your love smile before they see you:

♦ Send them a "Happy Wedding Day!" text message or a photograph of your wedding breakfast!

- Leave a card with some romantic words about the day somewhere they'll find it.

- Buy them a piece of jewellery or a token they can wear on the day, and have one of their friends deliver it to them in the morning.

- Organize for a horse and carriage or a fancy car to pick them up for the wedding (especially if they thought they were going in a taxi).

A close shave

♦ If you're planning on being baby-smooth for the big day, make sure you get up in good time for a hot, steamy soak to open up those pores.

♦ By shaving earlier in the morning there'll be more time for any redness to go down and ample opportunities for your groomsmen to tell you if you missed a spot.

- Don't try a new shaving regime on the day – this is something you should have planned in advance.

- If you're feeling shaky with nerves, wait to shave – you don't want to look like you've lost a fight to a razor blade.

- Slap on the moisturizer afterwards to avoid a rash and to leave your skin smelling divine.

Only once in your life,
I truly believe, you
find someone who
can completely turn
your world around.

♦ ———————— BOB MARLEY

*One word frees
us of all the weight
and pain of life:
That word is love.*

SOPHOCLES

Disaster dodger

If you're not staying at your own house, do a second check first thing in the morning to make sure you have everything you need and that your groomsmen are fully kitted out. If you realise early enough that something is missing, you can send a mate out to pick it up (a pair of matching socks, for example) – but leave it until five minutes before you're due to leave and someone's definitely going to have cold feet.

Enjoy the little things in life... For one day you'll look back and realise they were the big things.

◆ ——————— KURT VONNEGUT

Notes

Looking good

It can be hard to relax and enjoy your day if you're worried about how you look – especially when you know you'll be the centre of attention! So, shore up your confidence by avoiding the rookie errors such as greasy hair, dirty shoes or missing cufflinks, and learn all the tips on how to wow.

Being married does make a difference. It's a comfort, almost like someone holding your hand.

♦ —————— BRENDA BLETHYN

Suits you

———◆———

♦ Make sure your outfit has been pressed professionally at the drycleaners and is hung covered and uncrushed in a wardrobe. Let the suit breathe the night before and press any outstanding creases carefully if required. Don't go crazy with a hot iron and ruin your brand new suit. A crease always trumps a burn hole. Tell your groomsmen to do the same, especially if you've splashed out on suits for them.

♦ It's all in the details – a shirt that fits and sits flat against your body, a quality silk handkerchief, a pair of bright orange socks that tie in with the flower arrangements. Don't leave anything to chance by assuming it will all look OK on the day. Invite your buddies round for beers and try on your outfits the week before the wedding so you're confident everything ties together as you imagined.

Looking sharp

- Keep your shirt in place with braces (or tuck the tails into your pants for that taut appearance).

- Make sure you've clipped and cleaned your nails (especially if you're going to wear a wedding ring) and that you've addressed any facial manscaping, paying particular attention to errant nose and ear hairs!

- Don't put your jacket on until you reach the ceremony to avoid creasing the back of it on the sofa at home or in the car.

- Brush your teeth before you leave the house.

- Make sure you leave enough time to have a few photographs taken before you leave for the ceremony.

*The most beautiful
things in the world
cannot be seen
or even touched;
they must be felt
with the heart.*

◆ ———————— HELEN KELLER

Spit and polish

If you've never been to a regimental private school or joined the army, polishing your shoes is something you might rarely do. Expensive leather shoes – the kind of which you might have purchased precisely for this occasion – require the utmost respect and attention. Take note...

Tools:

Two quality brushes (one stiff, one softer), a cloth duster, and wax polish that matches the colour of your shoes (obvious, but an easy mistake!), shoe trees or newspaper

Steps:

1. Take out the shoelaces and clean any obvious dirt off the shoes – this can be done with a damp cloth.

2. Put in shoe trees (or some scrunched up newspaper) to stretch out the shoes.

3. Using the cloth or the stiff brush, apply a small amount of polish in circular motions to the whole shoe, including the tongue and heel.

4. Leave for two minutes for the leather to absorb the polish.

5. Buff using the softer brush and your biceps!

6. Pop the shoes on and buff again using the cloth in a sawing motion for a spectacular shine.

Don't forget... bits and buttonholes

♦ As uninterested as you might have been in picking out the wedding flowers, your buttonholes will make the groomsmen's outfits so don't forget to remind everyone to put them on.

♦ If you're not great at fiddly jobs, ask someone else to fix your buttonhole for you as they are delicate and can easily be damaged.

♦ Make sure the groomsmen's ties/cravats and handkerchiefs are neatly positioned to avoid looking scruffy.

♦ If you have them, sentimental cufflinks (such as your father's or grandfather's) make a great finish to a dress shirt.

Love does not consist of gazing at each other, but in looking outward together in the same direction.

♦ ANTOINE DE SAINT-EXUPÉRY

Disaster dodger

If you are inclined to wear a little fake tan on your big day, you must plan this into your schedule for the few days leading up to the wedding, otherwise there's a good chance your bright white shirt will end up with tan stains. Use a tried-and-tested product and give it a few days to settle. Remember not to go overboard – there's a fine line between a beautiful glow and an orange beacon.

◆ ———————————— *Notes*

Groomly greetings

As the groom, you have the pleasure of arriving at the ceremony venue first, settling into your surroundings, greeting the officiant and some of your guests, and setting the tone for the day. These tips will help you to make the most of those precious first moments of the big event.

Meeting and greeting

Don't be shy. More than anything, weddings are truly their best when all the guests feel relaxed and like one big happy family. This comes largely from how you react. When you see guests arriving at the venue, greet them, smile and wave. Even if you don't know someone, they are probably a relative or friend of your partner, so make them feel welcome.

*When love exists,
nothing else matters.*

ISABEL ALLENDE

Official business

When you talk to the officiant before the formal proceedings begin, make sure you raise any last-minute concerns about the order of events, the vows, the rings or the music. They will be able to put your mind at ease, and chatting to them informally first will make the wedding itself feel that much more intimate and relaxed.

Before the ceremony

♦ Sip bottled water and have breath mints to hand before the ceremony starts, especially if it's a hot day. Mints are preferable to gum so you won't find yourself unintentionally chewing during the event.

♦ Ensure your groomsmen earn their keep by handing out programmes and ushering people to their seats. They can also be responsible for fielding questions from other people at the venue.

Happiness, not in another place but this place... Not for another hour but this hour.

WALT WHITMAN

Stand tall

Once you've made your way into position for the start of the ceremony, follow these steps so you don't look like you're having second thoughts.

- Stay seated until you're told that your partner is nearly ready to make their entrance.

- If you do want to stand, try to plant your feet with weight distributed evenly on both feet.

- Don't keep looking to the back of the room – it will make you look nervous and uncomfortable.

- Chat quietly with your groomsmen, but try not to be too boisterous.

- Subtly check your fly is closed.

- Traditionally, the groom doesn't turn to see their partner until they're standing beside him at the front, but if you choose to break with tradition, stick with your choice and watch them walk the entire way to meet you.

Don't forget...

Because you arrive first, you can see to it that everything is just as it should be. If you haven't had a big hand in the planning, get instructions ahead of time as to what should be in place so you know what to expect and so you can fix any last-minute problems before the ceremony starts.

Never tell a secret to a bride or a groom; wait until they have been married longer.

◆ ————————— E. W. HOWE

Disaster dodger

There's nothing worse than offending one of your in-laws before the wedding has even begun. Make sure you are always with your best man and tell him there are a few relatives whose names you're a bit iffy on. If someone comes over to wish you well before the ceremony, assuming that you know who they are when actually you don't, introduce your best man immediately in an agreed way so he will know to ask the person's name, avoiding any embarrassment.

Notes

Pomp and ceremony

No matter what happens, you will remember this part of the day for the rest of your life: the vows, the music, signing the register, walking down the aisle as a married couple — here's how to do it all with ease.

Respecting the venue

Weddings are celebratory affairs, but they are also serious matters – both legally and spiritually. Everyone's views differ, but it is often the happy couple who set the tone for how everyone else behaves. If you're marrying in a place of worship, respect the space you're in and encourage your guests to do the same. If you want a more relaxed approach, it might be advisable to be married in a non-religious setting.

Love is friendship
set to music.

JACKSON POLLOCK

Keeping it together

♦ Look into your partner's eyes when they reach the front of your wedding venue – the whole atmosphere will be overwhelming, but the familiarity you share will help calm both your nerves.

♦ If you are doing a reading, remember to take slow, deep breaths, and speak loudly and clearly so all of your guests can enjoy it.

- Make sure you know which finger is the ring finger, and when it comes to that part of the ceremony, gently place it on rather than forcing it.

- If your partner has walked down the aisle with a loved one, acknowledge that person with a hug, a handshake or a smile.

This done, he took the bride about the neck, and kiss'd her lips with such a clamorous smack, that, at the parting, all the church did echo.

◆ —— WILLIAM SHAKESPEARE

True love doesn't come to you; it has to be inside you.

JULIA ROBERTS

Don't forget...

Kissing for the first time as a married couple can cause problems for some. The following pointers will ensure your smooch goes swimmingly.

- Grab hold of each other and get close – you're married now, so there doesn't need to be a big gap between you.

- No sudden movements – you don't want to butt heads, teeth or noses, so go in nice and slow.

- Keep your eyes closed while you kiss – it will look better in the photos.

- Don't practise beforehand – the best kisses are the most natural ones.

- Remember where you are and who you're kissing in front of. Be it in a church, in front of your grandmother or the officiant, remember to keep it PG – X-rated kisses are what the honeymoon is for.

Vows with pow

♦ If you are repeating standard vows,
  make sure you take your time to listen
  to the words the officiant is saying —
  these are the promises you're making
  to your partner, and you want to
  mean them, rather than robotically
  regurgitate them.

- If you're making additional personal vows, it's a good idea to have them written down – ask your best man to hold on to them and pass the paper to you at the appropriate moment.

- Look into each other's eyes as much as you can, even if you're reading vows.

- If your voice starts to waver or even if you begin to cry, take a second to gather yourself, rather than mumbling through the rest of your vows.

Marriage is the golden ring in a chain whose beginning is a glance and whose ending is eternity.

♦ ——————— KAHLIL GIBRAN

Blessed is the influence of one true, loving human soul on another.

GEORGE ELIOT

Disaster dodger

The signing of the register is an
important part of the wedding ceremony
– officially marking its place in the
history books. Ask friends or relatives
in advance if they will sign it for you so
that there's no awkward confusion. This
will also prevent anyone being offended
on the day for not being asked, causing
potential arguments.

Notes

Say cheese!

You've gone to all that trouble to look rather dapper, and your partner is as beautiful as the day you met them, if not more. Now it's time to make sure you have the ultimate keepsake from the day – a wonderful wedding album full of fantastic photographs.

Getting the most from your photos

- Be sure to get any photographs that include your guests out of the way first, so they can get on with enjoying the champagne and canapés while you are whisked off for a snapping session with your photographer.

- Make sure a trusted friend or relative is on hand with a pre-discussed list of all the various photograph groupings you would like. Although it's likely you will have discussed these with your photographer beforehand, a list will make sure no friends or relatives are left out.

- Smiling for all those photos could leave your jaw a little sore. Relax your expression after every few photos to avoid face ache and unnatural smiles.

- Make sure you're not photographed in direct sunlight – squinting is definitely not your best look.

- Don't obsess over how the pictures will turn out – trust your photographer and their experience and enjoy staring lovingly into your other half's eyes.

- Why not take a few "selfies" of you and your other half in between the photographer setting up shots for some extra-special memories you can post online throughout the day.

The whole point of taking pictures is so that you don't have to explain things with words.

ELLIOTT ERWITT

When you're lucky enough to meet your one person, then life takes a turn for the best.

◆ ———————— JOHN KRASINSKI

Posing masterclass

- Natural smiles are best, so let the photographer make you laugh.

- Make sure you remove all items from your pockets before the photographer starts – keys, phone, wallet, etc. No one wants to see unsightly bulges in their wedding pictures.

- Don't thrust out your chest to try and make yourself look bigger – it will only serve to make you look uncomfortable or unnatural. Instead, put your arms behind your back, pull your shoulders back and relax.

- Find useful places for your hands to go so they don't look silly – in your pockets, round your partner's waist, holding their hand, etc.

- You look dapper, so feel it too and your confidence and joy will shine through in your pictures.

Love is a flame: —
we have beaconed
the world's night.

RUPERT BROOKE

What I like about photographs is that they capture a moment that's gone forever, impossible to reproduce.

◆ —————— KARL LAGERFELD

Don't forget...

Have the following items to hand while you're having your photos taken:

- Tissues (in case you get emotional, or if you "get something in your eye")

- Comb (if your hair requires it)

- Your best man (if you want someone to help hold things for you like a bag or a jacket, etc.)

- A glass of champagne (optional!).

A photograph can be an instant of life captured for eternity that will never cease looking back at you.

◆ ———————— BRIGITTE BARDOT

Disaster dodger

If your partner is fussing over you before and during the photographs, let them. They want you both to look your best, because they know you'll both be enjoying these pictures for the rest of your lives. If anything, it's evidence of how much they love you. Let them fuss and adjust – you'll be grateful to look good in the long run.

Notes

A grand reception

Some grooms spend hours and hours poring over wedding blogs to find the perfect venues, decorations and dinner menu for their big day. Some... do not. Whether you're satisfied with your work or completely surprised, this will be an evening to remember for the rest of your life.

Prioritizing your time

With all the friends and family around it's easy to spend your entire day chatting with everyone but your other half. Make sure you find each other throughout the night and not just to pose for cameras.

Depending on how many guests are at your wedding, you will have an awful lot of people to meet and greet. Spend more time with your guests at their tables, rather than in a formal receiving line, by starting the dinner first and then greeting people one table at a time between courses. This gives them the opportunity to congratulate you, take your picture and see your outfits up close without the pressure of a moving line.

Here are fruits, flowers, leaves and branches, and here is my heart which beats only for you.

◆ ——————— PAUL VERLAINE

Enjoying the reception

♦ As much as you might want to have a quick make-out session in the car, don't leave your guests waiting too long – people will be hungry and don't want to hang around for hours.

♦ If you want to freshen up your hair or make any changes to your outfit, do this before entering the reception venue. Once you're there it will be really hard to tear yourself away from friends and family.

♦ Be sure to comment on how fantastic everything looks and shower your partner with compliments (especially if they happened to do more of the planning than you!).

Don't forget...

A good wedding planner will make sure all the elements of your wedding come together and are appreciated by your guests. In the absence of one, check off the following when you arrive at your reception venue:

- Have all the decorations/flowers/furniture you ordered arrived?

- Have all the appropriate place cards, party favours and centrepieces been added to the tables?

- Is the seating plan positioned where guests can see it?

- Have the tables been named or numbered correctly?

- Do the guests know the bar policy?

- Is there a clear timetable for the staff regarding drinks, food and entertainment?

- If you are having any entertainment, has it arrived? Are there any problems?

- What is the schedule for any musical elements to the reception?

Food for thought

◆ Remember that if you're planning on showing your partner a good time in the bridal suite, go easy on those triple servings – you don't want to end the night in a food coma.

◆ Enjoy the food, but eat gracefully with a large napkin across your lap to defend yourself against unsightly stains.

- Save room for cake! Your cake is never going to taste as good as on your wedding day. If you're a dessert person, this might be something you spent hours picking out so make sure you're not too stuffed to enjoy some!

- Follow each glass of alcohol with a full glass of water to stay hydrated and to ward off the more unglamorous effects of drinking.

*You cannot touch
love, but you feel the
sweetness that it pours
into everything.*

HELEN KELLER

Disaster dodger

More and more couples are choosing outdoor wedding reception venues, which can be magical and make for great photos. What doesn't look so great, however, is sunburn. If you're prone to burning, make sure you've brought a high-factor sunscreen with you to reapply throughout the day, otherwise your photographer will have to Photoshop red blotches out of your wedding album.

It is not the quantity of the meat, but the cheerfulness of the guests, which makes the feast.

◆ ———————— EDWARD HYDE

*If you fall in love
with their eyes, you'll
be in love forever.*

ED SHEERAN

Notes

Toasts and cake

You survived the walk down the aisle,
the first kiss, the grand entrance – but
now comes the real test: the speeches.
Soak up the love and pride of your guests
and the sweetness of your cake, and be
prepared for the occasional cringe!

Keeping the toasts in check

♦ Have those people giving the speeches stand beside the cake table – it makes for a lovely backdrop for photographs, and means that the whole room can be addressed, including those at the top table.

♦ It's a good idea to keep speeches to a minimum, and a time limit, otherwise guests can become restless. Break speeches up with dinner courses, music or a slideshow.

♦ Cut your cake immediately after the speeches when you have everyone's attention and all your guests are still present.

The best man's speech

+ The key to good wedding toasts is timing and organization. If your best man is giving a speech, and you're worried that things could go awry, assign a friend to keep an eye on how much he's drinking during dinner to avoid the toasts turning into a second stag night. A good way to avoid this is to make sure the toasts take place fairly early on so there's less chance of a blotto best man.

♦ If your best man delivers his speech and keeps it tame and teary, make a special mention of him in your own toast. If he decides to leave taste and decency at the door, keep a cool head, blush approvingly and recount an equally shameful story about him to the bridesmaids at the bar, especially if he thought he might be getting lucky later on.

The first dance

If you're having a first dance, wait until the wedding cake has been cut and served to your guests – that way they have something to nibble on while you're strutting your stuff.

Don't fancy having your dancing skills on display? Avoid the first dance by inviting everyone onto the dance floor immediately after the cutting of the cake.

Let us celebrate the occasion with wine and sweet words.

PLAUTUS

Don't forget...

It's traditional for the groom to say a few words, and even if you're the shy type it will mean a lot to your partner and their parents. Whether you, your partner or both of you choose to make a speech, ensure that someone remembers to thank the following people:

♦ Both sets of parents, where appropriate, especially those who contributed to the cost of the wedding

- The maid of honour, best man, bridesmaids and groomsmen, and give them any token gifts you have bought

- Any flower girls or pageboys

- Your wife's family for being so welcoming and for coming to the wedding

- Any other friends or family who have contributed significantly to the wedding (e.g. making the cake, doing the flowers, etc.).

In all of the wedding cake, hope is the sweetest of plums.

DOUGLAS JERROLD

I was the best man at a wedding one time... If I'm the best man, why is she marrying him?

♦ ——————— JERRY SEINFELD

Surprise, surprise!

If you're planning on surprising your partner on the big day, make sure you squeeze it into the proceedings seamlessly (after the toasts and cake-cutting is a good idea). Wait till your guests are eating cake and you'll have their undivided attention.

- Why not showcase your sexy dance moves with a choreographed performance with your mates, or sing your partner a song you wrote especially for the wedding?

- If you fancy blowing your partner's mind, hire their favourite band to play (and tell them they were unavailable in the build-up to the day) or pay for a celebrity they love to record a personalized message of congratulations.

- A really personal surprise sure to melt any newlywed's heart would be a video montage of photographs of the two of you throughout your relationship, with their favourite song playing in the background.

Think only of my love and that I am yours always and ever.

HENRY JAMES

Disaster dodger

When it comes to the age-old tradition of feeding each other from the first slice of wedding cake, it's easy to get carried away (after a few glasses of champagne) and want to initiate a food fight. Your partner might be all smiles now, but be warned – very few people want their cake in their hair, so stick to a friendlier approach if you want to stay in your new spouse's good books.

*Cakes are special...
Every celebration
ends with something
sweet, a cake, and
people remember.
It's all about the
memories.*

◆ ———— BUDDY VALASTRO

♦ ———————————————— *Notes*

Party time

Toasts and treats done, it's time to gossip, gulp and gyrate the night away with friends and family, and – most importantly – the love of your life!

A successful marriage requires falling in love many times, always with the same person.

◆ —— MIGNON McLAUGHLIN

Making your exit

You don't want to be one of the last people on the tiles, but equally you don't want to miss out on the party you're paying for. If you're not staying at your reception venue, have your mode of transportation ready to pick you up about an hour before the planned end of your reception. Then you have the option to have a proper send-off with all your guests before they leave, or to stay a little longer if the party is going strong.

Music expresses that which cannot be put into words and that which cannot remain silent.

VICTOR HUGO

Sharing the load

Make sure you and your partner aren't left doing any of the heavy lifting at the end of the night. Arrange for family members or friends to take charge of transporting any wedding gifts, centrepieces and leftover wedding cake, so you can head to your post-nuptial love nest worry-free.

The life of the party

♦ If you have extra guests arriving just for the evening, make sure you go out of your way to greet them and socialize with them on the dance floor.

♦ If the DJ isn't playing the music you agreed on, or you think your guests would appreciate something different, don't be afraid to ask – it's your party!

- Golden oldies and dorky dance moves may seem cheesy, but they'll get everyone on their feet, feeling comfortable and having fun.

- If you've organized any late-night food, such as a finger buffet or a food truck, make sure your guests know about it, otherwise you could end up leaving with your new spouse and a car-load of sausage rolls.

Those who danced were thought to be quite insane by those who could not hear the music.

◆ ——————— ANGELA MONET

Love is the master key that opens the gates of happiness.

OLIVER WENDELL
HOLMES SR

Don't forget...

◆ Weddings can turn into quite raucous
affairs, depending on the crowd – but
that's not for everyone. Be considerate
of your in-laws and keep an eye on
your friends' behaviour if you want to
make a good impression.

- Hanging out with your mates is a blast, but you do it every Saturday night. Make sure you're including other people in the fun, especially those who might have come on their own.

- Stay sober enough to say goodbye to anyone who heads off early (and so that you can carry your partner over the threshold of your hotel room!).

Opportunity dances with those already on the dance floor.

♦ —— H. JACKSON BROWN JR

Dancing is the poetry of the foot.

JOHN DRYDEN

Disaster dodger

If there are a number of children attending your wedding, it's a good idea to start the dance proceedings with more kid-friendly songs (or even allocate a separate space in the venue for a kids' party). This way they'll tire themselves out early and avoid being accidental victims of a crowded dance floor later in the night.

♦ ─────────────── *Notes*

Honeymooners

Your wedding was the day of your dreams, and now that it's all over you'll likely feel exhausted, poor and perhaps a little deflated. These tips will make sure you have a spring in your step long after the honeymoon suite.

Life goes on

- For some couples who already live together, own a house, have children and share bank accounts, not much will change after the wedding is over, but it's still important to make time to celebrate this exciting transition in your lives as a couple. Organize a dinner party with close friends, book your honeymoon or a weekend away, and start making plans for your home and your future.

♦ Boring as it may seem after planning the party of the century, you might want to start thinking about your financial situation: bank accounts, life insurance, pensions and your savings. You also might want to write a will (if you already have individual wills these should be rewritten now you're married). These might be things you've avoided before, but there's no time like the present to cement yourself as a married couple.

The calm after the storm

Don't panic if you don't have sex on your wedding night – it's quite common to pass out after such a long day and all that partying. It doesn't mean you love each other any less, and remember: there's always the morning after and the rest of your lives for the good stuff.

If you're not leaving for a honeymoon immediately, enjoy a few days together relaxing, taking long walks and steamy showers, and avoid feeling the post-wedding blues by reminiscing about the big day and opening your gifts.

Don't forget...

The wedding may be over, but there could still be a few things to tick off your to-do list:

- Paying any invoices for wedding goods and services

- Having your wedding outfits dry-cleaned

- Helping your partner to change their name, if they've chosen to, or changing your names together, with all the relevant organizations (banks, credit card companies, doctors, the tax office, your driver's licence and passport)

- Packing for the honeymoon and making last-minute activity bookings

- Chasing up the photographer and/or videographer for the pictures and video from the wedding.

How to honeymoon

♦ Don't put too much pressure on the honeymoon to be the most amazing time of your lives. Chances are it will be fantastic, but too much pressure for lots of sex, exceptional hotels and perfect weather can cause disappointment.

♦ Mention you're on your honeymoon everywhere you go — you never know what freebies are on offer to lovebirds.

- If your partner wants a bit of alone time on the honeymoon, it doesn't mean they've gone off you already – it's healthy to spend a bit of the holiday apart, especially if you found planning the wedding stressful. Do the same by getting into a good book, going for a run or chatting with the locals.

- Book a special activity in advance to surprise your love (e.g. scuba-diving or salsa lessons, or a surprise meal).

Thanking
your guests

♦ Create an invite-only file-sharing depository online using a site like Dropbox or Google Drive for all your nearest and dearest to upload and share any pictures they took.

♦ If you have a wedding website, send out a general message to everyone thanking them for coming.

Chains do not hold a marriage together. It is threads, hundreds of tiny threads, which sew people together through the years.

◆ ———— SIMONE SIGNORET

Disaster dodger

Don't start married life on the wrong foot: create a spreadsheet to keep track of all the wedding gifts, buy some thank-you cards and a bottle of wine, and have a quiet night in on the sofa writing them together. Just be sure not to squish your hard work if things start heating up between the two of you.

*Will you come
travel with me? Shall
we stick by each other
as long as we live?*

WALT WHITMAN

Notes

Wedding Tips for Brides

Verity Davidson

978-1-80007-696-9

Hardback

Wedding Tips for Brides presents ingenious ideas for any bride-to-be. Taking you through every stage – from the night before right up to the honeymoon – it's full of helpful tips, smart ideas and disaster dodgers to ensure that your wedding day is the magical, memorable event that you've always dreamed of.